THE BUSINESS OF
FANCYDANCING

THE BUSINESS OF FANCYDANCING

Stories and poems by Sherman Alexie

Hanging Loose Press
Brooklyn, New York

Published by Hanging Loose Press
231 Wyckoff Street
Brooklyn, New York 11217

Printed in the United States of America

Hanging Loose Press thanks the Literature Program of the New York State Council on the Arts for funding in support of the publication of this book.

Cover photograph by Carolyn Wright, courtesy of the Southwestern Association on Indian Affairs, Inc. Special thanks to Jocelyn Lieu and Chuck Wachtel.

Photo of the author by the Wellpinit Watchdog

Some of these poems first appeared in the following publications: *Aethelon: A Journal of Sports Literature, The Beloit Poetry Journal, The Black Bear Review, Caliban, the Chiron Review, Deep Down Things, Hanging Loose, The Journal of Ethnic Studies, New York Quarterly, NRG, Slipstream, Thirteen, Wind Row, Z Miscellaneous,* and *ZYZZYVA.*

The author thanks the Washington State Arts Commission for a grant in support of the writing of this book.

17 16 15 14 13 12

Library of Congress Cataloging-in-Publication Data

Alexie, Sherman
    The business of fancydancing / Sherman Alexie.
       p.   cm.
    ISBN 0-914610-24-4 (hard cover) : — ISBN 0-914610-00-7 (paper)
    1. Spokane Indians—Poetry.   I. Title.   II. Title: Business of fancy dancing.
    PS3551.L35774B87   1991
811'.54—dc20   91-35048
                                                                         CIP

 Produced at The Print Center., Inc., 225 Varick St., New York, NY 10014, a non-profit facility for literary and arts-related publications. (212) 206-8465

Contents

I Distances

II Evolution

III Crazy Horse Dreams

Introduction

Sherman Alexie's territory, as he describes in these forty poems and five stories, ranges from the All-Indian Six-Foot-And-Under Basketball Tournament to ESPN to the politics of geography and family to powwows to Indians "not drinking enough." Alexie's work has escaped the pervasive influence of writing workshops, academic institutions and their subsidized intellect, and has instead focused on reservation and border realities in his eastern section of Washington state.

Central to this landscape inhabited by family, friends, and a wild coterie of reservation cops, seers, Buffalo Bills, Crazy Horses, and of course, fancydancers, is the absence of self-indulgence. The characters in Alexie's work have actual identities whose faces have shadows that suggest other histories. The visionary Seymour and Simon, for example, travel forward and backward in time with dreams that sustain the narrator—often, they are Crazy Horse dreams and do not work, but sometimes they do, in a fancydance that suggests an existence beyond the survival of life's pain and contradictions.

Throughout this collection, there is an emphasis on balancing carefully, and a willingness to forgive, as in the subsistence forays into the sestina in "Spokane Tribal Celebration, September, 1987," and "The Business of Fancydancing." The history these stories and poems remember goes beyond the individual; it is the healing that attends the collective space and distance of both writer and reader, which will hopefully "make everything work/so everyone can fly again." Here, on a long jumpshot arcing into the distance, there is enough light to push back the darkness for several generations to come.

Alex Kuo
Changchun, China
August 1991

For my family, and for John, Spike, and Kari.

I
Distances

Traveling

My eyes were closed tight in the reservation November night and the three in the morning highway was the longest in tribal history. It was my father driving the blue van filled with short Spokane Indians, back from the Kamiah All-Indian Six-Foot-And-Under Basketball Tournament.

Orofino, Lapwai, Lewiston, Rosalia, Spangle, all the small towns miles apart, all the Indians in the bars drinking their culture or boarded up in their houses so much in love with cable television. I wasn't there when the old Indian man from Worley said it, but I know it must be true: Every highway in the world crosses some reservation, cuts it in half.

I was awake, listening to the sleeping sounds of the other Skins, to my father talking to his assistant coach, Willie Boyd, both trying to stay awake, afraid of the dark.

"Willie, I'm getting too damned old for this."

"We'd win more games if we could hit our free throws, enit?"

"Yeah, maybe. I guess we need to find a couple more players. Arnold gets tired, you know?"

"Shit, he's young. When I was his age I was the toughest god-damned Indian on the reservation, don't you know?"

"No way, I lived next door to you. Shit, you weren't even the toughest Indian on the block, enit?"

And they laughed.

It was hunger made me move then, not a dream, and I reached down and rummaged through the cooler for something to eat, drink. Two slices of bread, a half-full Pepsi, melting ice. My hand was cold when I touched my father's arm.

"Hey, Dad, we ain't got any food left."

"What's in your hand?"

"Just two slices of bread."

"Well, you can have a jam sandwich, enit?"

"What's that?"

"You just take two slices of bread and jam them together."

Willie laughed loudest and looked back at me.

"You can have a wish sandwich, too," Willie said. "All the time you're eating, you wish there was something in your sandwich."

All the talking stories and laughter woke up the rest of the Skins and my brother, two hundred and eighty-pound point guard, sat up and farted.

"Hey," he said. "I'm hungry."

It was on Highway 2 just before Reardan when the State Trooper pulled the blue van filled with Spokane Indians over to the side of the road. The Trooper walked up to my father on the driver's side cool and sure, like he was ordering a hamburger and fries or making a treaty.

13

"Excuse me, officer, what's the problem?" my father asked.

"You were weaving back there. Been drinking much?"

"Ain't had any, officer. Just coming back from a basketball tourney."

The Trooper held us all in his flashlight for a moment, held the light a little longer on the empty cooler.

"What was in that?" he asked.

"A whole lot of wishes," Willie said and we all laughed.

The Trooper took my father's license and the registration card and walked back to his cruiser. I watched him walk back in the headlights, taillights, moonlight, all pushing back a small circle of darkness.

"We all going to jail, enit?"

"Only if being Indian is illegal."

"Shit, being Indian has been illegal in Washington since 1972, don't you know?"

"How do you know that? When were you born?"

"1972."

We were still laughing when the Trooper came back to the van.

"Mr. Victor, I'm going to have to ask you to step out of the vehicle."

"Why?"

"Mr. Victor, I'm going to have to ask you to please step out of the vehicle."

"I didn't do shit."

"Mr. Victor, I won't ask again."

My father climbed out and we watched as the Trooper made him walk a straight line, touch his nose with his eyes closed, sing the Star Spangled Banner.

"Who holds the major league record for most home runs in a single season?" the Trooper asked my father.

"Roger Maris."

"No, it's Babe Ruth. You must be drunk. Who shot J.F.K.?"

"It wasn't Lee Harvey Oswald."

"Wrong. Who invented velcro?"

"You did."

The Trooper bumped chests with my father, spit in his face as he yelled.

"Now, you understand, Indian. Who is the most beautiful woman in the world?"

"Your mistress."

"Yes. Who is the greatest entertainer of all time?"

"Frank Sinatra."

"Perfect. What would you order with your bagel?"

"Cream cheese."

"Definitely. Never lox. Now, the last question. Are you now or have you ever been a member of the Communist Party?"

"No, no."

All the Indians were silent in the blue van as it climbed up the roads leading home to the Spokane Indian Reservation. I tore up

14

my two pieces of bread and passed it around to the other Skins.

Then, the blue van shuddered, the headlights went dim, out, and the van stopped dark in the endless night.

"What the hell is it?"

"Out of gas."

"Shit, we're going to have to push it home."

We climbed out of the van while my father and Willie sat in the front, watching the road. Ten skinnyspit Indians pushed hard while my brother struggled against his weight, against all of our weight.

"I'm so damned tired," he said, stopped pushing, stood still. I looked back as he stood on the reservation highway. I turned back to the van, put my shoulder to the cold metal and waited for something to change.

1.

I cut myself into sixteen equal pieces
keep thirteen and feed the other three
to the dogs, who have also grown

tired of U.S. Commodities, white cans
black letters translated into Spanish.
"Does this mean I have to learn

the language to eat?" Lester FallsApart asks
but directions for preparation are simple:
a. WASH CAN; b. OPEN CAN; c. EXAMINE CONTENTS

OF CAN FOR SPOILAGE; d. EMPTY CONTENTS
OF CAN INTO SAUCE PAN; e. COOK CONTENTS
OVER HIGH HEAT; f. SERVE AND EAT.

2.

It is done by blood, reservation mathematics, fractions:
father (full-blood) + mother (5/8) = son (13/16).

It is done by enrollment number, last name first, first name last:
Spokane Tribal Enrollment Number 1569; Victor, Chief.

It is done by identification card, photograph, lamination:
IF FOUND, PLEASE RETURN TO SPOKANE TRIBE OF INDIANS,
    WELLPINIT, WA.

3.

The compromise is always made
in increments. On this reservation
we play football on real grass
dream of deserts, three inches of rain

in a year. What we have lost:
uranium mine, Little Falls Dam
salmon. Our excuses are trapped
within museums, roadside attractions

totem poles in Riverfront Park.
I was there, watching the Spokane River
changing. A ten-year-old white boy asked
if I was a real Indian. He did not wait

for an answer, instead carving his initials

into the totem with a pocketknife: J.N.
We are what we take, carving my name
my enrollment number, thirteen hash marks

into the wood. A story is remembered
as evidence, the Indian man they found dead
shot in the alley behind the Mayfair.
Authorities reported a rumor he had relatives

in Minnesota. A member of some tribe or another
his photograph on the 11 o'clock news. Eyes, hair
all dark, his shovel-shaped incisor, each the same
ordinary identification of the anonymous.

4.
When my father disappeared, we found him
years later, in a strange kitchen searching
for footprints in the dust: still

untouched on the shelves all the commodity
cans without labels—my father opened them
one by one, finding a story in each.

Distances

I've been thinking about pain, how each of us constructs our past to justify what we feel now. How each successive pain distorts the preceding.

*

I picked up the phone because it was ringing.
"Do you know who you are talking to?" the voice on the other end asked.
"No," I said.
"Then you must have the wrong number," the voice said and hung up.

*

Have you ever decided to love someone because they loved you first?

*

I've watched the Children of The Third World starving on television. I've heard the standup comic ask, "Why didn't the cameraman give that kid a fucking sandwich?" I know all the mothers of America have told their kids: "Clean up your plate. There are people starving in India." When I was young, living on the reservation, eating potatoes every day of my life, my mother would tell me to "clean up your plate or your sister will get it."

*

A woman writes to a man who used to live here. I write back, pretending I'm the man she's been searching for her whole life. "Do you still love me?" she writes to ask him, and me.

*

I do not speak my native tongue. Except that is, for the dirty words. I can tell you what I think of you in two languages.

*

EDWALL, WASHINGTON — 186,000 miles

*

There is nothing as white as the white girl an Indian boy loves.

*

A photograph: Trina Andrews, reservation girl, nine years old, in a wheelchair, legs useless because of cancer, wearing a wig because of the baldness induced by chemotherapy, holding a bag of Christmas goodies, Santa Claus hovering over her; a dozen kids surrounding her, all staring into the lens, back at me and you. In that bag: an orange, a handful of peanuts, a few hard candies, and miles and miles of air.

*

My friend, Steve, told me this once: "All the girls I've ever loved should have their faces on the backs of milk cartons."

*

Remember this: "Electricity is lightning pretending to be permanent."

*

I was in a bar, drinking a beer, because it was filling the glass, when a stranger walked in.

Translated from the American

Agnes drove the senior citizens' van from powwow to powwow, watching all of her grandmothers sift into the even motion of earth, until she came to sit beside me, holding my son, her grandchild, as we drove west for The Spokane Tribal Celebration.

"He still has blue eyes," she said. "Only newborns are supposed to have blue eyes."

She studied my face for a reaction. I felt it darken by halves.

"When are they going to change?" she asked.

It was the only solid question between us, the last point after which we both refused the exact.

"They're always going to be blue," I said. "You know that."

"I have this dream all the time," she said, ignoring me. "I'm sitting with your son. He's in his crib and he keeps crying. But when I talk to him or sing to him, he grows. Really, he grows until he fills the room and I have to cut off one of his legs to get out the door."

Agnes touched my son's leg with the tip of a forefinger and whispered a word in Salish.

"What did you say?" I asked.

She repeated it, again in Salish.

"In English, you know I don't understand."

"It doesn't make any sense that way," she said.

I began to count mile markers, made mental lists of everything I really needed: a new pair of shoes, a winter coat for the baby, a ticket for a Greyhound traveling back or ahead five hundred years.

At that time of year, the end of summer, the last powwow, our skins returned reluctantly to our bodies. We could only come back to our half-life of four walls, old blankets, and black-and-white television. All the gifts from a thousand cousins buried in the trunk, used only once and forgotten. I laughed at the Flathead who gave us the electric blanket in Arlee, a town of random electricity and occasional water. I asked him what he remembered and he said half of everything that ever happened to him.

"Pretty damn good percentage," I said in my mind, then aloud.

"What?" Agnes asked, though I knew she heard me. She enjoys repetition as a form of tradition.

"That old man in Arlee said he remembered half of everything that ever happened to him. I think that's a good percentage," I said.

"That's nothing," she said. "I remember everything."

"Really?" I asked her. "What's my son's name?"

She called him by a word in Salish.

"That's not his name," I said.

"It's the one I gave him."

"It's useless," I said, only half-believing it. Years ago, when Agnes tried to teach me the language, she told me to hold a smooth stone in my mouth, under the tongue. She would say the words for salt, pepper, mother, son, and I would try to repeat the Salish exactly, until my tongue blistered around the stone. Ashamed of my voice when I could not say the words, I would hide for days in the trees, stealing food from the kitchen in the middle of the night.

"His name is Joseph," I said.

"White name," she said.

"He's half white," I said. "I thought you remembered everything."

"I remember you leaving us to be with the Catholics. I remember you coming to visit us with your books of lies, when you told me you could speak German. I remember you were so proud you knew a foreign language. I remember I told you English was your foreign language and you left again."

"It was college," I said, but she had nothing more for me, either too many memories for her to classify or not enough words for her to be specific. She held Joseph tightly against her chest, despite me, and watched the landscape move toward her, beside her, and then away.

The road sign read WELLPINIT–HOME OF THE 99TH ANNU- AL SPOKANE TRIBAL CELEBRATION–25 MILES. I found myself following a line of cars, followed by a longer line of cars, all travel- ing to the same place, all leaving from another. In some small, ordi- nary way, Indians are still nomadic, always halfway.

We pulled into Wellpinit, another reservation town of torn shacks and abandoned cars. We found the powwow grounds and stopped at the entrance. The Indian deputy, a cousin of the Tribal Police Chief or a Councilman, leaned into our open window.

"This here is a dry powwow," he said. "You don't have any alco- hol or drugs in the car, do you?"

"No," I said. "We don't have anything except us."

Morphine and Codeine

What was it you told me about your pain?
That you wanted me to take it, shake its hand
and walk it down to the hospital cafeteria
for lunch, while you watched television
for an hour or two, able to laugh cleanly?

That night I slept in the cot next to your bed
and the fire alarm went off for some reason
and you jumped to the floor, too surprised
to remember you didn't have the strength
to walk, why did you call me Jackson SunDown?

What vague shadow of my face fit his?
Did he speak the language? Did he fancydance
while all the Indian princesses took
his picture and kept the polaroids taped
to the walls of their rooms? After we buckled

you down, the nurses and I, you looked straight
at me, your eyes like x-rays. Did you see
the hairline fracture running along my jaw?
The fracture that happened the summer I called
myself Running Eagle, unaware of the contradiction,

and leapt from the roof of your house, my arms
flailing insanely as I landed on the woodpile.
Do you remember the ride in the ambulance,
the pain-killer they gave me? I want it to be the same
they give you now, but I'm not sure it was. I'm not

sure of very much of that small part of my life,
the moment I remember now, barely, because
it was the first time I took any medicine other than yours,
the last time you wrapped me in old blankets
much too big for anyone with the smallest possible dreams

like myself, who dreamed you learned a new language
after they took your vocal cords, who dreamed
your hands tapped a strange code against my skin
so I knew what you were thinking, who dreamed for years
of cancer, that loup garou, that house fire and ash.

Grandmother

old crow of a woman in bonnet, sifting through the dump
salvaging those parts of the world
neither useless nor useful

she would be hours in the sweatlodge
come out naked and brilliant in the sun
steam rising off her body in winter
like a slow explosion of horses

she braided my sister's hair with hands that smelled deep
roots buried in the earth
she told me the old stories

how time never mattered
when she died
they gave me her clock

The Fausto Poems

1.
Talk story, he said.
He said, talk story.

2.
He said, I'm more than American
        my grandfather fished off cliffs
        before Hawaii was a state.
        I'm more than Hawaiian
        my mother is Filipino
        my father Japanese.
He said, I went to school in the same building
        all my years. I went to church
        and named myself Catholic.
        I wanted to go to college
        in a place where it snowed
        where the ocean did not reach.

3.
Spokane, Washington, is 186,000 miles away
from your four walls and bed, I told him.

He told me, that's the speed of light.

A little girl asked him once how many hours
the drive from Hawaii took on a good day.

He told me, I just blinked my eyes.

4.
The first night it snowed, Fausto
woke me up at three in the morning
throwing snowballs at my window.
He stood, knee-deep in white, wearing
only his underwear and a San Francisco 49ers hat.

5.
On Thanksgiving I took him home
to my reservation and he wanted to ride horses.

I don't know how to ride, I told him.

He said, I thought all Indians rode horses.

On Christmas, we watched ESPN surfing

and I asked him how well he rode the waves.

He said, I don't know how to surf.

I thought all Hawaiians surfed, I told him.

6.
In the woods behind my house, Fausto
stood under a hundred-foot tall pine tree
watched the snow falling off the branches
with the wind, the ordinary motions of earth.

It's like cold sand, he said.
He said, it's like cold sand.

7.
We both needed money
so we applied for dishwashing jobs
in the student dining hall.

We both showed up late
for the interview.
Neither of us was hired

and when I asked him
why he was late
he said, I was taking my time.

When he asked me
why I was late, I told him
I was taking my time.

8.
When he did not talk, he would point
to say "hello," "goodbye," "eat,"

and then he would push me into walls
to say "shut up," "go away," "no."

He would talk long-distance on the phone
pointing out the words "mother," "father," "home."

9.
He said, he was tired at two
in the afternoon, so tired
he wanted to sleep all night long
wake up at two the next day.

He said, he felt so old
with every day, so old
he wanted to find his way home
and become his grandfather.

I would knock on his door, asking
Are you there? Are you still there?

10.
He left school in the middle
of the night, left his clothes
and his best pair of shoes.

All one summer, I called Hawaii
long distance at three in the morning
but it was always the wrong number

or a disconnected line
or a busy signal
or his mother and father answered

to tell me Fausto was working
in a canning factory, working
in the graveyard shift seven days a week.

I stayed up late every night
to watch reruns of Hawaii Five-O
Magnum P.I., The Don Ho Specials

looking for his face
in the crowd, his hands large
and torn, fisherman's hands.

11.
Then, this letter from Kentucky
        from North Carolina
        from No Return Address

Fausto a PFC in the U.S. Army
sitting in his green uniform
with the flag in the background.

He writes, I fix helicopters.
He writes, I make everything work
so everyone can fly again.

Sudden Death

Down past the tracks in the tin shack
where the television keeps the walls
breathing, my father dreams of 1956

and the field goal he missed in the snow,
ball bouncing off the upright, falling
back to the tattered couch where my father throws
a spiral across the room, suspended

between the sound of a glass thrown
and a glass shattering against the corner. My father
roaring past the fourth quarter like a train

leaving a lover behind, stands eagle-armed
on the platform, whistling for God and 1956
to pick him up, carry him on their shoulders.

Penance

I remember sun-
days when the man I
call my father made

me shoot free throws, one
for every day of my life
so far. I remember
the sin of imperfect

spin, the ball falling in-
to that moment between
a father and forgive-

ness, between the hands reach-
ing up and everything
they can possibly hold.

House Fires

The night my father broke
the furniture and used the pieces
to build a fire, my mother tore me
from my bed at 3 a.m. Eyes and mouth

wide with whiskey, she told me
we were leaving that place
and would never come back.
We drove for hours, under the gates

of this reservation, as she recanted
years of life with my father,
the man who pulled
our house from its foundations
and sent us all tumbling down

to a cafe in Colville. We took penance
in the breakfast special, she told me
she forgave all our sins. We drove back

to my father, gathering ash
in his hands, planning to bury it all
in the graves we had chosen for each other.

November 22, 1983

"we were doing laundry
when we heard it on the radio
& your father changed

the channel to some station
still playing music
& he asked me to dance
& we two-stepped

my heart beating
Dallas Dallas
your father held me

against his thin chest
for twenty years whispering
'ain't no Indian loves Marilyn Monroe' "

Love Hard

Hookum, jug-in-a-brown-bag man,
when it's time to plant your garden
in a Mexican shirt and baseball hat,
do you remember your friends back
on the Coeur d'Alene Indian Reservation?

"I'm not going home this year
for the basketball tournament," you tell me.
"Because I know too damn many drunks
and I've been on the wagon for two months
this time, three months the time before."

Driving through reservation farmland
with my father and I, you are more
than the man who keeps us company, who waits
in the car while the BIA processes our checks.
"I remember your father when he was the wildest

Indian boy on the reservation," you tell me.
"He would drink all night long and wake up
in the morning hitting jumpshots from thirty feet
until forever. Your dad would score twenty points
in the first half, drink a six-pack at halftime

and then score twenty more in the second half."
Hookum, you tell me the same old stories
my father has been telling me for years
a memory like news clippings, but I want to know why
my wild pony of a father never died, never left

to chase the tail of some Crazy Horse dream?
"Your father always knew how to love hard,"
you tell me, crawling over broken glass, surviving
house fires and car wrecks, gathering ash
for your garden, Hookum, and for the old stories

where the Indian never loses. In my father
I'll find the hard edges of the earth
where I was raised, dust
thin and unforgiving, time and God and beer
following us in rows.

Transient

For Kari

If it was your face I saw
only once, I would remember you
as the beautiful stranger I saw
only once, on the Greyhound
shuttling past me at 2 a.m.
in the city where I chose to live

alone for months. Strangers answered doors,
would not let me enter their homes
wearing my own good clothes. I had to change
the shovel-shape of my incisors, disguise
shadows that wandered beneath my eyes.

There is nothing that can demand itself
the exact way sleeplessness demanded
your presence on the streets, a shadow
I could never change or redefine
in some simple way. I always felt
your wrists pressed against my chest

as I lay under newspapers, pulling
old clothes from shopping carts and paper sacks
like a street magician making dimes appear
in the hands of generous tourists. I wept
dimes into quarters and made a living

on the corners. I played four-string guitar
for dollar bills tucked into a wine glass.
I gave all my blood to the plasma center
hoping for enough to get bus fare back home.
Wearing new clothes and dark hair, I sat
at the depot watching all the buses roll out

east to Chicago past all the small towns
miles apart. Single lights in windows flared
as I reached my hand out from the pane
of this bus where I once saw your face
almost, dreamed of running along the rails

reaching for the last train traveling back
to the simple dress you wore. I could feel
my eyes breaking under the wheels of the train
shuddering through all the tunnels between
those empty places, where grey men sat

on wooden crates around solitary fires. I sang

the blues like an old black man done bad,
my hands wrapped around the harp, blowing
night air back into lungs of the lonely
red-faced men who gathered around me in circles.
I wandered the world other people call Seattle

and dreamed of mirrors centered
on the walls of your room, I walked
up to those mirrors and saw myself as you might
see me if I were to stand in your window
at midnight. You played the piano for me, softly
touching the keys as if they were skin.

You stood to greet me as I entered your room
dissonant and foreign. I gathered ash
from the road I'd traveled, placed it at your feet.
You led me to the window that could take in
the whole landscape or the fine edge

of a flower petal on fire.
We raised our arms to the wind, silently
my mouth was surrounded with words
I could never speak
alone. We had come together
to call this space arched in our backs home.

When I Die

call the cooks
the old Indian women
who cook for every wake
buried to their elbows
in flour and lard
laying out flat
the bread the plates

"anee," the old ones scream
they weep like herons

pack up all my possessions
give them to mourners
waiting in line
give my bedding
to the thin-chested
give my clothes
to children without shoes
leave my house
only its windows

"enit," we say when we want it
we want it all

bury me alone
in old blankets

"bones," we whisper in stick game
we all get to choose

Futures

oh children think about
the good times — Lucille Clifton

We lived in the HUD house
for fifty bucks a month.
Those were the good times.
ANNIE GREEN SPRINGS WINE
was a dollar a bottle.
My uncles always came over
to eat stew and fry bread
to get drunk in the sweatlodge
to spit and piss in the fire.

No one never had no job
but we could always eat
commodity cheese and beef
and Mom sold her quilts
for fifty bucks each to whites
driving in from Spokane
to buy illegal fireworks.

That was the summer I found
a bag full of real silver dollars
and gave all my uncles all
my brothers and sisters each one
and no one spent any   no one.

Dead Letter Office

I get a letter, written in my native tongue, but I don't understand it, so I spend the night searching for a translator, until I find Big Mom in the bar. She speaks the language, but I have to fancydance for her, in blue parka and tennis shoes, circling the jukebox, while all the other Skins fall back to the floor, from whiskey and fear and sex and dreams, calling me by a name I recognize but cannot be sure is my own, until closing time, when Big Mom rises from her chair, walks out the door, and I follow her for years, holding some brief letter from the past, finding she had never been here, she had never gone.

II
Evolution

Special Delivery

Thomas Builds-the-Fire told his story to every other Skin on the Spokane Indian Reservation before he was twelve years old. By the time he was twenty, Thomas had told his story so many times all the other Indians hid when they saw him coming, transformed themselves into picnic benches, small mongrel dogs, a 1965 Malibu with no windshield. Eventually, Thomas could only find audience with the half-assed Indians, passed out behind the tribal trading post. Thomas leaned over, whispered his story to these Indians, who dreamt the words true and woke up hours later, rubbing their ears until they grew out of proportion.

Thomas Builds-the-Fire woke up at precisely 6:30 every morning, stood in front of his bathroom mirror and repeated his story, practiced the words again and again. *This is my small ceremony*, Thomas thought as he dressed, combed his hair into braids, washed his face. At 9:15 every morning, Thomas left his house and traveled to the post office on the hill, looking for some response to all the letters he mailed, an 8½ by 11 measurement of his story.

Thomas Builds-the-Fire wrote letters to congressmen, game show hosts, invited the president of the United States to his high school graduation. Every word Thomas used in his letters was part of his story; every word was exact and essential.

* * *

Thomas waited outside the post office, stamping his feet against the cold. He tried the door, still locked, peered through the front window, looking for Eve, the reservation postmaster. The clock on the wall inside the post office read 9:30. Thomas checked his watch, found he had the same time.

"You're late, Eve," he whispered, looked down the road he had traveled, the road leading down the hill into Wellpinit, the only town on the reservation.

Wellpinit. The HUD houses sat down in neat rows, the roads paved and straight, even a few feet of cement sidewalk here and there, but the government surveyors had only guessed at the possible routes of travel, completely neglecting the politics of geography.

Sitting in the Powwow Tavern one Friday night, Thomas had listened to Simon explaining the politics of time, distance, and geography.

"You see," Simon said, "there's point A, and that's where you are, and then there's point B, and that's where you're supposed to be. So it's how you get from point A to point B, how long it takes you to do it, and what you see along the way, that is politics."

"I'm drunk now," one of the Andrew brothers yelled out from the back of the bar, "and I plan on being drunker later."

"My friends," Simon said, "point A is drunk. Point B is drunker.

That's politics."

Thomas smiled at his memory of Simon talking a good story, smiled more fiercely when he saw Simon come driving down the road in his pickup, weaving from one side of the road to the other.

Simon drove off the road, ran over a shrub, jumped a curb into the trading post parking lot, and parked directly behind Mary Song's station wagon. Mary climbed out of her car, waving her arms and cussing so loud Thomas could hear her all the way up the hill at the post office.

"Goddamn, Simon," Mary yelled. "I ain't got time to wait for your crazy Indian ass. Get your goddamn truck out of the way."

Simon jumped out of his truck, tipped his cowboy hat at Mary, and walked into the trading post. He walked like he spent his whole life riding a fat horse, so bowlegged he spent more time moving side-to-side than he did walking forward.

"Might as well drive like I walk," Simon had explained to Thomas one night. "I wouldn't want any Skins to think I was some stranger driving around town."

Most days, Simon could be spotted in his Chevy pickup weaving his way down the reservation road. The tribal police just waved and shook their heads whenever Simon drove on by.

"I drive this way sober," Simon said, "and the cops will never know when I'm driving drunk as a skunk."

Thomas was still laughing to himself when Simon walked out of the trading post with a bag of groceries in one arm. Mary Song cussed some more as Simon tipped his cowboy hat to her again, jumped in his truck, backed up out of her way, kept on backing up, out of the trading post parking lot. Simon backed onto the main road, still driving in reverse, weaving back and forth, still backing up until Thomas could no longer see the pickup in the distance.

When Eve, the reservation postmaster, drove up the hill, Thomas was still laying on the ground, laughing, holding his stomach in pain. Eve stopped her car, looked at Thomas twitching on the ground and wondered for a moment if it was some kind of seizure. *No such luck*, she thought as Thomas sat up, wiped his eyes, and called out.

"Ya-hey," he said. "You're late this morning."

Eve climbed out of the car, walked past Thomas without comment, and unlocked the front door of the post office. Thomas followed her inside, watched as she threw her purse and keys into a corner and flipped on the lights.

"Eve," Thomas asked. "You got a few stamps I can have? I'm out."

"No. I told you yesterday. Nothing is free anymore."

Thomas looked around the post office, examining each detail. Eve watched his eyes scanning the room.

"Thomas, this place never changes. Why are you always checking it out like it was new?"

"First time I been here today. So it's like starting all over."

Eve walked up close to Thomas. She stood over a foot shorter, the top of her head barely reaching Thomas mid-chest.

"Well, Thomas, if it's like starting all over, why don't I answer all your questions before you ask the same damn things."

Thomas stepped back, surprised at the knowledge in Eve's voice.

"No," she continued. "You can't have a few envelopes, no bite out of my sandwich, no drink out of my Pepsi, no long walks in the moonlight, no dollar bills for wine, no nothing."

Thomas found he had no voice as Eve turned her back and busied herself with a large stack of U.S. Government mail: form letters, income tax returns, Indian Health Service Bulletins. THE AMERICAN INDIAN AND DIABETES. ALCOHOLISM AMONG THE IN-DIGENOUS PEOPLES OF THE AMERICAS. THE IMPORTANCE OF VITAMIN C.

Thomas stared hard at the curve of Eve's back, searching his mind for the words which would describe the movement of blouse over skin. Only one word came to his mouth: treaty. But he bit the word back, refusing any belief in promise.

"This isn't right," he said.

"What isn't right?"

"This isn't how the story is supposed to be."

"I don't know what the hell you're talking about."

"I'm talking a story," Thomas said, hoping Eve would remember the part she played.

Every morning, Thomas walked into the post office at 9:25 and Eve would look up from sorting mail.

Every morning, Thomas asked the same question: *Does Custer deliver the mail now, Eve? I'm tired of waiting.*

Every morning, Eve answered the same way: *I don't write the letters, Thomas. Come back tomorrow.*

"This isn't right," Thomas repeated, leaned over the counter, into the air surrounding Eve.

"Thomas, are you feeling sick? Maybe you should go see a doctor. Go home and get some rest, you know?"

Home. Thomas searched his memory for that word, home. Somehow, he knew it was wrong, deviating from his story in such a way that the air reversed itself as it came into the lungs.

"Sometimes," he said, "it's very hard to breathe."

"Listen, Thomas. How about I give you a ride to the clinic?"

"That's not what I mean," Thomas replied, staggered toward the door. *This is not my story,* he thought. *I do not belong here.*

He walked outside, leaving Eve to the mail, traveled back down the hill to the trading post. He stood by the garbage dumpster, checked his watch.

"I'm running late this morning," he whispered, drawing the attention of a black dog who ambled over and sat at Thomas's feet.

"Ya-hey," Thomas greeted the dog, "Buffalo Bill, my old friend, you're also running late this morning."

The reservation dog stared up at Thomas Builds-the-Fire, waiting to hear the story.

"Buffalo Bill, I remember many years ago when you were young and powerful and feared by all the Spokane Indians."

Thomas closed his eyes and the story came to him: "Late at night, standing around the woodstove, my father showed me his scars, the souvenirs from Buffalo Bill. My grandfather would also lift up his pant leg and display the same twisted calf muscle my father possessed. *He doesn't go for the kill,* my father said, *he wants to hurt you, to cripple you, and leave you with a permanent record of your trespasses and indiscretions.* Once, my father got down on all fours and growled deep in his chest. *This is how it happens,* he said and chased me from room to room, all our breath thick with whiskey and fear."

Thomas opened his eyes and looked down at Buffalo Bill.

"Do you remember?" he asked the reservation dog.

Thomas closed his eyes again, the story continued: "I was ten years old, sitting on the powwow fence with all the other Indian boys, watching all the princesses walk by. *Ya-hey,* I called out to them but could not be heard over the fancydancers, the drums, the drone of stick game, and tires breaking bottles against sawdust. I shouted to the princesses until my throat was too hoarse and tender beyond pain."

Thomas opened his eyes, kneeled down beside Buffalo Bill, held the dog tightly by its ears.

"Buffalo Bill, you must remember the Spokane Indians never ate dog meat."

The reservation dog shook free of Thomas, trotted over to the front door of the trading post and sat down next to the feet of Junior, the reservation autistic. Junior watched the automatic door open, close. He spent hours watching the door most days, more fascinated with the useless technology than autistically obsessed.

Thomas himself spent more than a few moments transfixed by the door, dissonant, like a missed step in a fancydance. All the Skins were still surprised when the door swung open on their approach. The door was a promise kept; the door was an instantly redeemable treaty.

"Simon," Thomas said to himself, thought of his friend. "Point A is this side of the door. Point B is the other side of the door. So, the door is politics."

Thomas smiled at his own small piece of wisdom, was still smiling when Simon swung his truck into the parking lot, still driving backward, and drove past the trading post into a utility pole.

Thomas, Simon, even Buffalo Bill and Junior, watched as the pole swayed slightly from side to side, gaining momentum like a reverse pendulum, back and forth in ever-widening arcs, until gravity pulled it down to the ground.

Sparks flew as the live wires touched, crawling along the grass like blind snakes. Simon was out of his pickup, waddling as fast as he could away from the wires, sidestepping, hopping on one foot, skipping.

"Ya-hey," Thomas yelled at Simon, "I didn't know you were a fancydancer."

Simon ran out of reach of the wires, stopped, and whooped.

"Thomas," he asked, breathing hard. "What does this teach you?"

Thomas searched his mind, could not find this lesson to be learned anywhere in his story.

"Simon, I don't know what this means."

"It's simple. Electricity is just lightning pretending to be permanent."

Simon sat down hard on the ground, watched the eye-level fireworks dancing around his truck. Thomas did not understand Simon's words. *This is not right*, Thomas thought, as he backed away from Simon, almost a stranger now.

"Ya-hey, Thomas. Sit down beside me and watch the show."

Thomas shook his head, repeated Simon's words to himself, could not recognize their meaning, confused the verbs with the color of Simon's shirt.

This is not my language, Thomas thought as he turned to run but stopped as he saw Buffalo Bill walking down the road beside Junior.

"Buffalo Bill," Thomas cried out. "You have not heard the rest of my story."

The reservation dog did not look back and Thomas fell to his knees. He watched the manager of the trading post pushing at the automatic door, frozen shut, without electricity.

Simon also watched the manager sweating, straining against the inevitable. Simon started laughing, laughing so hard he never saw the tribal police cruiser pull into the parking lot.

"What the hell happened?" the tribal cop asked loudly as he climbed out of his car.

"Goddamn Simon killed the utility pole," the manager of the trading post said between grunts, through the glass of the automatic door.

Simon stopped laughing when he heard his name. He looked up at the tribal cop with wide eyes. The tribal cop walked over to Simon, picked him up by his braids.

"Goddamn it, Simon," the tribal cop yelled. "You been drinking too much again?"

"Some of us drink too much. Some of us don't drink enough."

Thomas put his forehead to the ground, his behind sticking up into the clear morning sky. Simon started to laugh when he saw Thomas kowtowing but the tribal cop silenced him with a left uppercut to the jaw, sending Simon's upper plate into the air.

This isn't right, this isn't right, Thomas was chanting to himself when the tribal cop dropped Simon, unconscious, to the dust. Thomas was still chanting when the tribal cop walked over and picked him

43

up by his braids.

"What do you have to say for yourself?" the tribal cop asked Thomas.

Thomas looked at the tribal cop, this face that did not belong in Thomas's story. Thomas closed his eyes, invented a memory: "I was in fifth grade at the reservation school. Mrs. Aristotle was my teacher. Red hair, green eyes, she stood in front of the classroom, holding a pencil sketch I gave her as a gift. It was just a simple drawing of the tribal longhouse. *Class*, she said, *I want you all to take a look at some real talent.* I wanted to tell Mrs. Aristotle, to shout it in her face: *We are not the same color. We are not the same color.* She looked at me and she smiled, like she was giving me a gift instead of making me a sacrifice. *Thomas*, she said, *you have quite an eye for perspective for someone so young.* I pulled myself down into my chair, heard all the Skins in the classroom laughing, so I covered my head when they started throwing pencils, erasers, bottles of Elmer's glue, a Big Chief Tablet paper airplane, and dreams. I looked up at Mrs. Aristotle and searched her face for recognition of her sins, some evidence of my possible rescue. She came to my desk, leaned over, and her blouse dropped forward until I could see her small, white breasts hanging down into her bra. I sat there and waited for something to change."

Thomas opened his eyes, looked hard at the tribal cop.

"Is that all?" the tribal cop asked.

"It's all I can remember."

The tribal cop held Thomas off the ground with one hand while he made a fist with the other.

"I'm going to beat your ass, Thomas."

Thomas closed his eyes, not in fright, but in the hope that he would find something familiar when he opened them again. He counted one, two, three, opened his eyes and saw Eve hanging off the tribal cop's arm.

"Let him go, let him go," Eve screamed, holding tight to the tribal cop, distracted long enough for Thomas to break free and run.

Thomas broke into an easy stride. *Relax, relax,* he told himself, *breathe through your nose.* The tribal cop threw Eve to the dirt and started after Thomas.

"Thomas," he yelled, "get your Indian ass back here."

Eve sat on the ground, watched the tribal cop chase Thomas out of the trading post parking lot, up the hill toward the post office.

"That's my goddamn post office," she yelled, jumping to her feet and started after Thomas and the tribal cop. *Relax, relax,* she told herself, *breathe through your nose.*

Thomas was halfway up the hill when he checked his watch: 10:30. He looked behind him and watched Eve run past the tribal cop.

"That's my goddamn post office," she yelled, kept yelling as she gained ground on Thomas. They skidded to a stop at the front door of the post office simultaneously. Eve opened the door, Thomas ran through, Eve followed him, closed and locked the door.

Thomas bent over, his hands on his knees, dizzy. *Breathe deep,* he told himself.

Eve looked out the window just as the tribal cop made it to the top of the hill and slumped against the front door of the post office.

Breathe deep, the tribal cop told himself, *breathe deep.*

Thomas stood straight, looked around the post office, examined each detail. Everything was still the same here.

"Eve," he asked. "You got a few stamps I can have? I'm out."

Eve looked at Thomas, couldn't believe he was trying to start the morning at the very beginning.

"Thomas," she said. "Get your head out of your ass. The tribal cop is right outside the goddamn door and when he catches his breath, he's going to beat the crap out of you."

Thomas felt a sudden, sharp pain in his head. He pressed his hands tightly against his skull, wanting to keep his story from escaping, expanding the walls. *This is not right,* he thought, *my story is never supposed to change.*

Eve touched Thomas's arm and the usual static rose along the skin. She took him into her arms.

"Thomas, do you need a doctor? Do you need help?

Thomas closed his eyes and sank to the floor, pulling Eve down with him.

"This isn't my story," he said. "This isn't my story."

Eve was still holding Thomas when the tribal cop started pounding on the front door.

"Thomas," the tribal cop yelled. "Open the goddamn door, I got you surrounded."

Thomas jumped to his feet, sent Eve sprawling.

"Get the hell out of here," Thomas yelled back. "I've got a gun and I might use it."

The tribal cop started laughing, laughed until three other tribal cops pulled up in their cruisers. They all threw open their doors and crouched behind them, revolvers drawn, arms propped in open windows.

"Put those goddamn things away," the tribal cop yelled to his newly arrived partners. "You ain't the reservation SWAT team."

Thomas looked quickly out the window, saw the other tribal cops and dropped to the floor.

"Thomas," someone said through a bullhorn. "We know you ain't got a gun, come on out."

"Maybe I got the idea of a gun," Thomas yelled back. "And that's just as good."

"What the hell are you talking about?" Eve asked Thomas.

"I'm talking a story."

* * *

We interrupt regularly scheduled programming to bring you this special live report:

"In Wellpinit, Washington, the Spokane Tribal Police have surrounded the United States Post Office where Thomas Builds-the-Fire, age 35, an enrolled Spokane Indian, has allegedly held Eve Ford, age 36, hostage for over 8 hours with the idea of a gun.

"I have with me Tribal Police Chief David WalksAlong. Chief WalksAlong, how would you assess this situation?"

"Well, we're worried about what Thomas might think of next. He's always had a very good imagination."

"Has there been any communication with Builds-the-Fire?"

"Well, negotiations have been pretty much limited to possible changes in the weather, the cost of a stamp, and the politics of time."

"What exactly is the politics of time?"

"You see, Thomas started this morning at point A, and it took him about 9 hours to get where he is now, which is point B. What Thomas wants is to get rid of all that time in between point A and point B. You know, start the whole damn day at the beginning."

"Thank you, Chief WalksAlong. As you can see, the situation here is very inexact. Officials at the Bureau of Indian Affairs have declined comment. This is Andy Jackson, reporting live from Wellpinit, Washington."

* * *

The post office was cold and dark. Thomas wanted to start a fire with junk mail but Eve stopped him.

"That's a federal offense," she said, "and you're in enough trouble already."

She lay on the floor, wrapped in a mail bag, while Thomas sat with his back to the door, alternately closing and opening his eyes.

"Why do you do that with your eyes," Eve asked. "Ever since I've known you, you've done that with your eyes."

"I see better with my eyes closed. But I don't like much of what I see so I have to keep opening them to let in good light."

"So, tell me what you see now?"

Thomas closed his eyes, a new story came to his mouth: "When I was a baby, so much a baby I couldn't walk or talk, my head started to grow. Only my mother could see it happening, knew it was growing, but the doctors said *No, it was a mother's imagination growing.* My mother measured the size of my skull every day; it grew two inches in one week. She said my head was visibly growing. Each second became an explosion of possibilities. My mother read all the medical journals, stole textbooks from the Indian Health Service Clinics, and watched THE NATIONAL GEOGRAPHIC television specials. She found out some animals have to keep eating continually, grind their teeth down endlessly. *The teeth will keep growing,* my mother said, *if the animals don't grind their teeth down, they will grow into the brain and kill.* My skull was expanding, pushing outward, all the while changing my hearing and my vision, even changing the shape of my teeth. I was born with dreams, lies, lust, all impossibly large, filling my mind and spilling out onto the floor."

Thomas opened his eyes, looked across the room at Eve.

"Is that true?" she asked.

"Simon explained truth to me," Thomas said. "If there's a tree in the distance and you run to get there, run across the grass with all your heart, and you make it and touch the tree, press your face against the bark, then it is all true. But if you stumble and fall, lose your way, move to the city and buy a VCR and watch cowboy movies all the time, then nothing is true."

Eve and Thomas remained silent, silent, until David WalksAlong spoke through the bullhorn.

"Thomas, we don't think you have the idea of a gun at all. We're giving you ten seconds to get your ass out here or we're coming in."

"They're calling my bluff," Thomas said, stood, faced the door. "I better give myself up."

"No," Eve said. "They'll hurt you. They think you're crazy."

"What choices do I have?"

"I don't know. Tell them you have the idea of forgiveness, of survival, of something."

Thomas reached out for the door handle. Eve stood up to stop him but he waved her back.

"Eve, there's something about my story no one has ever heard. No one ever let me finish."

"What is it?"

"A long time ago, my vision animal came to me. He limped to me on three legs, carrying the fourth up close to his chest. He asked for a drink of water but I only had whiskey. He asked for deer jerky but I only had commodity cheese. He looked at me and said, *Thomas, you don't have a dream that will ever come true.* I've been waiting all these years for someone to tell me different."

Eve watched Thomas walk out the door, off government property, listened to the spaces between sound. *It isn't necessary,* she wanted to say, *it isn't necessary.*

Evolution

Buffalo Bill opens a pawn shop on the reservation
right across the border from the liquor store
and he stays open 24 hours a day, 7 days a week

and the Indians come running in with jewelry
television sets, a VCR, a full-length beaded buckskin outfit
it took Inez Muse 12 years to finish. Buffalo Bill

takes everything the Indians have to offer, keeps it
all catalogued and filed in a storage room. The Indians
pawn their hands, saving the thumbs for last, they pawn

their skeletons, falling endlessly from the skin
and when the last Indian has pawned everything
but his heart, Buffalo Bill takes that for twenty bucks

closes up the pawn shop, paints a new sign over the old
calls his venture THE MUSEUM OF NATIVE AMERICAN CULTURES
charges the Indians five bucks a head to enter.

At Navajo Monument Valley Tribal School

from the photograph
by Skeet McAuley

the football field rises
to meet the mesa. Indian boys
gallop across the grass, against

the beginning of their body.
On those Saturday afternoons,
unbroken horses gather to watch

their sons growing larger
in the small parts of the world.
Everyone is the quarterback.

There is no thin man in a big hat
writing down all the names
in two columns: winners and losers.

This is the eternal football game,
Indians versus Indians. All the Skins
in the wooden bleachers fancydancing,

stomping red dust straight down
into nothing. Before the game is over,
the eighth-grade girls' track team

comes running, circling the field,
their thin and brown legs echoing
wild horses, wild horses, wild horses.

Artificial Respiration

The old Indian man sitting next to him
in the Tribal Café falls face first into his dessert:

DOA.

He   cardio
finishes   pulmonary
lunch   resuscitation

Western Nuclear needs night help
to carry buckets of dirty water:
                       "Hey, Chief,"
says the white foreman
        "Now you'll be able to find your way
        when you stagger home from the bar
        in the middle of the goddamned night
        'cuz you'll be glowing in the dark."

Sometimes, it's easier to wake up with thoughts of forgiveness
pour a glass of milk and take a drink before you realize
it should have been sold by April and it's November now
but still you finish because it all tastes so familiar.

−OR−

You watch through your window
into your bedroom from the outside
your wife between the thighs
of another BIA official   she keeps
bringing him back to life.

It's all too much when trying to sleep
the lungs cannot hold all you have to swallow.

Powwow

YOU TOO CAN HAVE A PHOTOGRAPHIC MEMORY
yes, it changes itself in the dark
of a powwow three in the morning lust

the fancydancers wear bells, you know
so they can't sneak up on white tourists

what happens is this:
continuously, as if it could be solid
picked up from the dust like a coin, etc.

O, do you remember the little white girl
who came every year to sell turquoise
with her father, a huge rumbling imitation
of himself stranded in a wicker chair?

she sat on the powwow fence, blonde
skinnyspit ugly telling the tough Indian girls
the world ain't all tipi poles and fry bread

if you close your eyes and open them
again quickly, they will water

that's all it means

sometimes, the best story is the one that happens:

>Wanda walking into the outhouse, three hundreds pounds
>of naked summer, she sat down over the hole, the hole where
>Lester FallsApart had passed out again and fell down into,
>his hands coming up between Wanda's thighs like a B-movie,
>she getting up and running out afraid screaming in English
>and Indian, pants wrapped around her ankles, hands flying
>like toilet paper in the air

this isn't love exactly
it's love, approximately

of course, we all bring ourselves back
to beauty: twenty-dollar bills, bootleg
everything, a traditional dancer
from Montana who doesn't speak English

did you ever get the feeling
when speaking to a white American
that you needed closed captions?

suddenly, nothing happens

then, you stand bowlegged, leaning against
some video game or another watching the black girl
from Seattle who hitchhiked here by accident
and has spent all her quarters using the pay phone
that doesn't work, hasn't worked since 1876

now, you realize the importance of plastic
how it lasts forever, sometimes you think
a whole new generation of treaties is typed
onto the labels of household cleaners

today, nothing has died, nothing
changed beyond recognition

dancers still move in circles
old women are wrapped in shawls
children can be bilingual: yes and no

still, Indians have a way of forgiving anything
a little but more and more it's memory lasting longer
and longer like uranium just beginning a half-life

Independence Day

"It was the worst goddamn thing I ever saw," the Old Man tells me. "I was working out on the Reservation last summer. Fourth of July. The Smoke Shack was selling fireworks, had it all stored in the basement and about three in the morning, it explodes. Turned out some little Skin broke in, you know, and we guess he didn't want to turn on any of the lights, so he flicked his Bic and up it went. Anyway, we're sifting through the ash, before we even knew the kid was there, and I kick something. I look down and it's the kid, just his head. I yell over to one of the Tribal Cops and he comes over, picks the head up and boots it like a damn football, thirty or forty yards. Fucking kids, the Tribal Cop yells, walks back to his car, climbs in, and drives off. I couldn't believe it," the Old Man tells me. "I never thought a head could travel that far."

Indian Boy Love Song (#1)

Everyone I have lost
in the closing of a door
the click of the lock

is not forgotten, they
do not die but remain
within the soft edges
of the earth, the ash

of house fires and cancer
in sin and forgiveness
huddled under old blankets

dreaming their way into
my hands, my heart
closing tight like fists.

Indian Boy Love Song (#2)

I never spoke
the language
of the old women

visiting my mother
in winters so cold
they could freeze
the tongue whole.

I never held my head
to their thin chests
believing in the heart.

Indian women, forgive me.
I grew up distant
and always afraid.

Indian Boy Love Song (#3)

I remember when I told
my cousin
she was more beautiful

than any white girl
I had ever seen.
She kissed me then
with both lips, a tongue

that tasted clean and un-
clean at the same time
like the river which divides

the heart of my heart, all
the beautiful white girls on one side,
my beautiful cousin on the other.

Indian Boy Love Song (#4)

I remember when my father would leave,
drinking,
for weeks. My mother would tell me

the dream he needed
most
was the dream that frightened him
more

than any stranger ever could.
I
would wait by my window, dreaming

bottles
familiar in my hands, not my father's, always
empty.

Reservation Love Song

I can meet you
in Springdale buy you beer
& take you home
in my one-eyed Ford

I can pay your rent
on HUD house get you free
food from the BIA
get your teeth fixed at IHS

I can buy you alcohol
& not drink it all
while you're away I won't fuck
any of your cousins

if I don't get too drunk
I can bring old blankets
to sleep with in winter
they smell like grandmother

hands digging up roots
they have powerful magic
we can sleep good
we can sleep warm

Some Assembly Required

Gordie the Glazer making donuts,
saving money for professional wrestling school,
says a burglar broke into his house,
stole the toaster and nothing else.

Gordie says he doesn't have enough money
to buy a new one and he hates donuts
though they're free for employees,
so he goes without breakfast,

hungry until lunch hour
when his wife stops by
with a brown paper bag
filled with ham and turkey,

lettuce leaf, tomato slice, cheese.
Where the hell is the bread
Gordie asks his wife
and she says the burglar came back,

stole the bread and butter
while she was in the shower.
Gordie punches out, runs home
and sits in his kitchen

surrounded by small helpless appliances,
teaching his daughter card tricks,
watching the windows
waiting for something to happen.

Lottery

The Professor tells me he dreams, dreams of a bus station at the beginning of everything else, where another Indian tries to board the last Greyhound without paying fare, the same Indian hitchhiking in the rain no matter where you drive, and you stop, let him into your life, call him cousin, and take him anywhere he wants to go, passing through gates of some reservation, buying illegal fireworks, cigarettes, a raffle ticket for a '57 Chevy, and you promise yourself you can win that car, drive away, hide in a rest stop miles from anywhere red or white, or anything somewhere in between.

III
Crazy Horse Dreams

Father Coming Home

THEN   Father coming home from work. Me, waiting on the front steps, watching him walk slowly and carefully, like half of a real Indian. The other half stumbling, carrying the black metal lunch box with maybe half a sandwich, maybe the last drink of good coffee out of the thermos, maybe the last bite of a dream.

SPOKANE   Father coming home from work five days a week. Me, waiting every day until the day he doesn't come walking home, because he cut his knee in half with a chainsaw. Me, visiting my father laying in bed in the hospital in Spokane. Both of us, watching the color television until my mother comes from shopping at Goodwill or Salvation Army, until the nurses come in telling us we have to go.

CEREMONIES Father coming home from the hospital in a wheelchair. Me, waiting for him to stand up and teach me how to shoot free throws. Me, running up to him one day and jumping hard into his lap, forgetting about his knee. Father holding me tight against his chest, dark and muddy, squeezing his pain into my thin ribs, his eyes staying clear.

AFTER   Father coming home from the mailbox, exercising his knee again and again. Me, looking up from the floor as he's shaking his head because there is no check, no tiny miracles coming in the mail. Father bouncing the basketball, shooting lay-in after lay-in, working the knee until it bleeds along the scars. Father crying from the pain late at night, watching television. Me, pretending to be asleep. All of us listening to canned laughter.

INSOMNIA   Father coming home from another job interview, limping only a little but more than enough to keep hearing no, no, no. Me, eating potatoes again in the kitchen, my mother's face growing darker and darker by halves. One half still mostly beautiful, still mostly Indian, the other half something all-crazy and all-hungry. Me, waking her up in the middle of the night, telling her my stomach is empty. Her throwing me outside in my underwear and locking the door. Me, trying anything to get back in.

HOMECOMING Father coming home from drinking, after being gone for weeks. Me, following him around all the time. Him, never leaving my sight, going into the bathroom. Me, sitting outside the door, waiting, knocking on the wood every few seconds, asking him *Are you there? Are you still there?*

NOW   Father coming home finally from a part-time job.
                 Driving a water truck for the BIA. Me, waiting
                 on the front steps, watching him come home
early every day. Him, telling my mother when they think I can't
hear, he doesn't know if he's strong enough. Father telling mother
he was driving the truck down Little Falls Hill, trying to downshift
but his knee not strong enough to keep holding the clutch in. Me,
holding my breath. Him, driving around the corner on two wheels,
tons and tons of water, half-insane. Me, closing my eyes. Him, balanc-
ing, always ready to fall. Me, holding onto father with all my strength.

War All The Time

Crazy Horse comes back from Vietnam
straight into the Breakaway Bar,
sits down at the same table
he was sitting at two years earlier
when he received his draft notice.

Crazy Horse asks the Bartender for a beer
free, because he's some color of hero
although he doesn't know if it's red or white
because there are no mirrors in the bush,
only eyes tracing paths through the air,

eyes tearing into the chest, searching
for the heart. Crazy Horse sells his medals
when he goes broke, buys a dozen beers
and drinks them all, tells the Bartender
he's short on time all the time now,

measuring it leaning out car windows,
shattering beer bottles off road signs,
and when the Bartender asks him why
he's giving up everything he earned,
Crazy Horse tells him you can't stop a man
from trying to survive, no matter where he is.

Misdemeanors

The Old Man tells me he's a tough ex-con but his wife, the Waitress, tells me that he went to jail for robbing a bowling alley. The Old Man took off his shoes and used his socks to protect his hands when he punched through the window of the bowling alley, the Waitress says. He broke into the cash register but they only had coins, so he filled his pockets. He runs out to the getaway car but the driver had passed out. So here come the police and they find the Old Man barefoot, with his socks on his hands like gloves, and his pants hanging down to his knees because his pockets are full of pennies. So the police count all the change and it came out one cent short of a felony charge. He was in County Jail for six months. Thank God he wasn't trying to steal horses.

No Drugs or Alcohol Allowed

at the Spokane Tribal Centennial Celebration but Seymour is a
goddamned genius
and our native hero so he walks in first with an empty bottle
right past the guards
and then I take a big drink from a fifth in our car
outside the gate
but I don't swallow and I walk past the guards smiling a tight-lipped
smile holding the whiskey in
and then I spit it into Seymour's empty bottle and Lester follows me
doing the same thing
and after quite a few trips we have a complete fifth and I guess
you could say
we won again but it was only Indians versus Indians and no one
is developing a movie script
for that and it's too bad because I think Seymour looks exactly
like Charles Bronson
when he was younger and still multi-ethnic instead of a little man
with a big gun
but Seymour hates everything white so I don't tell him what I think
and we're too busy selling
drinks from our bottle for a dollar a shot which is good money
which is the kind
Seymour calls Crazy Horse Money and it means we can do
    whatever we want
and twenty dollar bills and hips
and stick game all mean the same thing
until we begin to sober up
and go broke which is exactly when Seymour decides to fight ev-
    ery white man
at the powwow
and there are dozens with cameras and a film crew from a local
    city
covering the events
for the local news so Seymour attacks them with a broken bottle
breaking it
again over the head of a prominent concerned reporter who files
a live report
highlighting the renewed rivalry
between whites and reds although
it's still the same because Seymour
alias Crazy Horse
gets the shit kicked out of him by a softball team from Spokane
all of them white
coming out to the reservation to win the softball tournament and walk
home with $1,000 prize money

but Seymour survives that only spends a night in jail and they
    don't even
put it on record because there is no law against Crazy Horse anymore
all of those
were written off the books
when he was killed a long time ago but white people don't real-
    ize he came
back to life
and started his own cable television channel and began the
    reeducation
of all of us who spent so many years
skinless, driving our cars straight off cliffs directly into
the beginning of nowhere.

The Business of Fancydancing

After driving all night, trying to reach
Arlee in time for the fancydance
finals, a case of empty
beer bottles shaking our foundations, we
stop at a liquor store, count out money,
and would believe in the promise

of any man with a twenty, a promise
thin and wrinkled in his hand, reach-
ing into the window of our car. Money
is an Indian Boy who can fancydance
from powwow to powwow. We
got our boy, Vernon WildShoe, to fill our empty

wallets and stomachs, to fill our empty
cooler. Vernon is like some promise
to pay the light bill, a credit card we
Indians get to use. When he reach-
es his hands up, feathers held high, in a dance
that makes old women speak English, the money

for first place belongs to us, all in cash, money
we tuck in our shoes, leaving our wallets empty
in case we pass out. At the modern dance,
where Indians dance white, a twenty is a promise
that can last all night long, a promise reach-
ing into back pockets of unfamiliar Levis. We

get Vernon there in time for the finals and we
watch him like he was dancing on money,
which he is, watch the young girls reach-
ing for him like he was Elvis in braids and an empty
tipi, like Vernon could make a promise
with every step he took, like a fancydance

could change their lives. We watch him dance
and he never talks. It's all a business we
understand. Every drum beat is a promise
note written in the dust, measured exactly. Money
is a tool, putty to fill all the empty
spaces, a ladder so we can reach

for more. A promise is just like money.
Something we can hold, in twenties, a dream we reach.
It's business, a fancydance to fill where it's empty.

Heroes

Drinking all night, with Lester FallsApart, he tells me the story about the time he spent in McNeil Island Prison for writing bad checks. I just played basketball all the time, he tells me. I went in there thinking all Indians could play ball, but the Skins in there were two hundred winter beers wide. Anyway, there was this old Skin named Silas Something-or-Other, always dressed up traditionally, braids and all. He never talked but everyone said he was a lifer, in for some serious shit, and I wonder to myself what he done to get life, so I walk up to him one day in the yard and ask him what the hell he did. Well, he says to me, during the war a few of us captured 20 Germans but we needed help, so the others left me to guard the prisoners while they went to rejoin the company and get relief. Shit, they must have got ambushed or forgot me or just plain left me because they never came back. After a few more days of staying awake, watching the Germans watch me, scared all to hell of falling asleep and those bastards getting loose, I slapped in a full clip and killed all those fucking Nazi bastards. I supposed I was crazy being so tired and scared because I kept shooting them, unloaded ten or twenty banana clips on them. When they found me, I was cutting off all kinds of body parts. I've been in a lot of places since then and now, I'm here, on the Island. That's fucked up, I tell Lester, and he agrees and we drink one for Silas Something-or-Other, the only medal he'll ever get.

Missing

for Spike Mulligan

What is lost is lost. — Ignace Paderewski

Crazy Horse gets a job at 7-11, four dollars an hour, graveyard
   shift

DOORS MUST REMAIN UNLOCKED
DURING BUSINESS HOURS

and all the Coke he can drink free. Crazy Horse picks up a
   nicotine habit
spends breaks lighting up in the cooler, hiding behind the milk
   and eggs
because his co-workers told him there's much less smoke that way.

WARNING: THE SURGEON GENERAL HAS DETERMINED
THAT CIGARETTE SMOKING IS DANGEROUS
TO YOUR HEALTH

Crazy Horse learns how to take inventory, decides his dreams
   have expired
have become so old they must be sent back to the distributor,
   recycled
and shipped to another city, a photo of Crazy Horse printed
   on each container.

AS LONG AS WINDS BLOW
GRASSES GROW AND RIVERS FLOW

Have you seen this man? A crazy woman from some
   reservation dials 911
again and again. She finds Crazy Horse in her mirrors, in the bar
near her house, fancydancing in the eyes and ears and mouths
   of Indian boys

NO INDIANS ALOUD

afraid of their hands, reaching for bottles, hips, government checks
every hour punched into their hearts, floating just above minimum.

Ceremonies

Seymour and I steal the Bartender's car and drive
down the Crazy Horse Highway
until an ice cream truck cuts us off and I'm halfway into the
twenty-third wreck of my life, Seymour yelling drive goddamn
   it, drive, we come to a stop in the middle
of a wheat field,
Seymour upside-down in the back seat while I study the exact
sculpture of my face smashed
into the glass of the windshield and Seymour asks me
if I'm dead yet and I say no
give me a beer, but before he can, an Asian man dressed in
black reaches
through the window and whispers something about his wife,
   missing
for years somewhere
near Minidoka, Idaho and then I recognize him he's the same
one who walks the reservation road
carrying six garbage bags filled with old clothes and shoes
he lines them up,
picks up the last one in line, walks it to the front,
   sets it down
next to the others
then walks back and picks up the last bag again, walks to the front
and sets it down again, over and over
for miles, doing it for years and he reaches back into the
window of the car asks me if I've seen his wife and I say no,
   but do you need a ride
somewhere, and he shakes his head
points in no direction at all but in the exact direction
he needs to go
and I understand that look in his eyes, his vision still cut by
   chain link fence
and dust and dreams,
the kind Seymour calls Crazy Horse dreams, the kind that
   don't come true
just like my father,
who lost a gold tooth in the forty-sixth wreck of his life
somewhere in Ford Canyon
and he spends a few hours every week with a metal detector,
scanning the ground
for that missing part, the part that came out whole and bloodless,
but fills you up with how much it stays gone.

Native Hero

I can never call the reservation home
or its water tower or the community center
where I play basketball every winter
measuring the decline of an Indian
by the number of points he scores

and when Reuben throws in 68
my white friends ask me why
he never played ball anywhere else.
I say he plays ball everywhere,
Nespelem, Worley, Plummer, Wapato...

He could be 25 or 45 I don't know
what he calls home except the roads
leading from reservation town to town
and maybe the basketball he keeps
tucked under his arm more gently

than any baby he may have fathered
when some Indian girl opened herself
to his reputation and memories
of his jump shot falling from the sky
into the bottom of the net, a salmon

hung out to dry for all of us
to tear into strips and eat,
sitting in the bleachers waiting
to watch Reuben play and never grow old.
We all keep those dice locked in our wrists

but Reuben rolls sevens everytime he shoots.
He is the man who knows the color of bones
in stick game. He is the man who never loses
a hand in poker or blackjack. He can drink
every other man under the table and still take

someone else's wife home. I can look him
eye to eye at the tip. We could be two snakes
entwined fighting for the ball. I know
no matter where it goes or what hand it chooses
I can never call the reservation home.

Spokane Tribal Celebration, September 1987

for Junior

This is the first powwow I
've been to in five years, night
falling like an old blanket
on shoulders of turquoise women
selling sawdust jewelry and dreams.
I want to believe every campfire

is a heart, every dollar bill a fire
that burns at the fingertips. I
'm walking with Seymour, his dreams
simple as smoke. "Tonight,"
he says. "I want all the women
to crawl under one big blanket

with me." He wears a colored blanket
for a coat, standing close to the fire
to get warm, all the old men
laugh and call him Joseph. He says, "I
don't have no brothers except this night
and the moon and this bottle of dreams."

Seymour swallows mouth after mouthful of dreams
until he believes his beautiful blanket
is a pair of wings. He says, "Tonight,
I'm going to fly through the pine like fire."
We all laugh, especially me, because I
know the only time Indian men

get close to the earth anymore is when Indian men
pass out and hit the ground. "My dreams,"
Seymour says, "are just like fry bread. I
heat them up and they rise." He wraps his blanket
close to his body, dancing around the campfire.
Someone says, "Seymour is sure drunk tonight.

He thinks he's a goddamn Indian." The night
and Seymour keep singing names of women
he loves: Jana Wind, Nadine WildFire,
Suzy Boyd, all the women every Indian Boy dreams
of sharing the dusty ground and a blanket
with. Seymour keeps singing and dancing and I

wonder if I and the other Indian men
will drink all night long, if Seymour's dreams
will keep him warm like a blanket, like a fire.

Eugene Boyd Don't Drink Here Anymore

The Stranger walks into the bar, orders a beer, and asks me where the hell Eugene Boyd is, and I tell him, he got shot last year in the parking lot of the Gold Coin, man, he's dead. The Stranger looks me in the eyes, looks the whole bar straight in the eyes, and drinks his beer in one drink. Who the hell did it, the Stranger asks me, and I tell him that everyone knows but the police ain't going to do anything about it because when one Indian kills another Indian, that's considered natural selection. He holds that empty glass tight and looks in the mirror behind the bar where all our faces are reflected. All us stoic Indians rehearsing for parts as extras in some eternal black and white western. Shit, used to be only whites expected Skins to have monosyllabic faces, but now, we even expect it of each other. But the Stranger looks in the mirror and he starts crying. Crying for the dead, not looking forward to the gifts he'll get from the deceased, not looking forward to the wake, he's crying for the dead. I used to figure strength was all a matter of being waterproof, like our houses could never be. So the Stranger throws his glass at the mirror, shattering us all into pieces, and in the silence after that the Professor, at the end of the bar, tips his beer and says, "that was some serious fucking dualism."

The Reservation Cab Driver

waits outside the Breakaway Bar
in the '65 Malibu with no windshield.

It's a beer a mile. No exceptions.

He picks up Lester FallsApart
who lives in the West End
twelve miles away, good for a half-rack.

When congress raised the minimum wage
the reservation cab driver upped his rates
made it a beer and a cigarette each mile.

HUD evicted him
so he wrapped himself in old blankets
and slept in the front seat of his cab.

When the BIA rescinded his benefits
he added a can of commodities for every mile.

Seymour climbed in the cab
said, this is a hell of a pony.
Ain't no pony, the reservation cab driver
said, it's a car.

During the powwow, he works 24 hours a day
gets paid in quilts, beads, fry bread, firewood.

3 a.m., he picks up Crazy Horse hitchhiking.
Where are you going, asks the reservation cab driver.
Same place you are, Crazy Horse answers
somewhere way up the goddamn road.

Basketball

After a few beers here, every Indian is a hero of "unbroken horses." Someone always remembers I was the Reservation point guard with the Crazy Horse jump shot. Someone always wants to go one-on-one in the alley while Lester FallsApart balances on a garbage can, his arms forming the hoop. Someone always bets his ribbon shirt against mine, and we play, and I win. Someone always finishes the night bareback, like it should be, while I go home, hang another shirt in my closet, another Crazy Horse dream without a skeleton or skin.

Giving Blood

I need money for the taxi cab ride home to the reservation and
I need a taxi
because all the Indians left this city last night while I was
    sleeping
and forgot to tell me
so I walk on down to the blood bank with a coupon that
    guarantees
me twenty bucks a pint
and I figure I can stand to lose three or four pints but the
white nurse says no
you can only give up one pint at a time and before you can do
    that
you have to clear
our extensive screening process which involves a physical
    examination
and interview
which is a pain in the ass but I need the money so I sit down
at a wooden desk
across from the white nurse holding a pen and paper and she
    asks me
my name and I tell her
Crazy Horse and she asks my birthdate and I tell her it was
    probably
June 25 in 1876 and then she asks my ethnic origin and I tell
    her I'm an
Indian or Native American
depending on your view of historical accuracy and she asks me
my religious preference and I tell her I prefer to keep my
    religion entirely independent
of my economic activities
and then she asks me how many sexual partners I've had and
I say one or two
depending on your definition of what I did to Custer and then
she puts aside her pen and paper
and gives me the most important question she asks me
if I still have enough heart
and I tell her I don't know it's been a long time but I'd like to
give it a try
and then she smiles and turns to her computer punches in my name
and vital information
and we wait together for the results until the computer prints
a sheet of statistics
and the white nurse reads it over a few times and tells me I'm
sorry Mr. Crazy Horse
but we've already taken too much of your blood
    and you won't be eligible
to donate for another generation or two.

Pawn Shop

I walk into the bar, after being gone for a while, and it's empty. The Bartender tells me all the Indians are gone, do I know where they went? I tell him I don't know, and I don't know, so he gives me a beer just for being Indian, small favors, and I wonder where all the Skins disappeared to, and after a while, I leave, searching the streets, searching storefronts, until I walk into a pawn shop, find a single heart beating under glass, and I know who it used to belong to, I know all of them.

Gravity

What is it that requires an Indian man to remember every other Indian he's ever met? I've read the human being only uses 10 percent of the brain's capacity. The Indian must use the remaining 90 percent to store the names of the Flathead who lent him twenty bucks in Arlee, the Crow woman a thousand miles from home who called him beautiful, every single entry in the reservation encyclopedia.

Every Indian has the blood of the tribal memory circling his heart. The Indian, no matter how far he travels away, must come back, repeating, joining the reverse exodus. There are no exemptions, no time to pull off the highway for food, gas, lodging.

I sit in the driveway, listening to the sounds of my car's engine cooling, settling. The HUD house throws bright squares of light out of its windows, making Indian shadows on the lawn.

How long have I been gone?

The clock on the dashboard reads 3:30 a.m., but it's been at least four years since I looked at a clock. There must be a new language for measuring time.

What have I forgotten?

I've been here before sitting in the driveway watching the windows of this HUD house, waiting for an Indian to stand in profile. At this distance, with my eyes, it would be impossible to distinguish individual features. Instead, it would be a sense of an Indian, the knowing who it was without the formalities of sight.

There, it could be my father standing in the window, smoking a big cigar. I can see the small flame when he lights the Havana that Alvin Horse mailed him C.O.D. from Florida. I can see the reflection of the flame in his U.S. government glasses. I can smell the smoke.

I look again at the clock on the dashboard, dismiss that illusion. I tap the odometer, hoping for a vision of all the miles.

When does the warranty expire?

Someone, an Indian, is standing in the window again, looks out toward my car. I can hear the engine cooling. It must be my father who opens the window, leans out, nearly falls.

"Ya-hey," he calls out. "We were wondering when you were coming back home."

He is sitting at the kitchen table, in the house alone, his wife and daughters, my mother and sisters, off to a powwow in Colville. His right eye is perfectly white and frightening against his brown skin.

"What is it?" I ask him.

"Glaucoma."

"How bad?"

"At night, I can't see a damn thing. During the day, I can see only half of everything, no matter how fast I turn in circles."

"You know, I never meant to be gone this long."

He looks up at me, all my attention is focused on his blind eye, wanting to know what new kind of vision has come to him, if it's an x-ray that can steal your bones, if it's a see-through-the-lies organ, if it sucks in all the available light, jealous of what it cannot use but refusing to share.

"I kept track of you," he tells me. "Bet you didn't know that, did you?"

"No."

"I got an old friend in Seattle who sent me newspaper clippings. I know about everything you did over there."

"Everything?"

"Yes, I got the complete illustrated history of Chief Victor, Junior, in paperback and hardback. I'm negotiating for the television rights."

He smiles at his own joke. He has Indian teeth.

Sometime later, after an interval, he walks into his bedroom and comes back with a scrapbook. He hands it to me with his palms facing up, and I take it without reservation.

"What is this?" I ask.

"It's not empty."

I look at the cover of the scrapbook, my name embossed in blue, a photograph of me at some age or another in the center. Is history this easy? Watch the newspapers for changes in the weather, the stock market, the standings in the National League West, the lottery numbers. Paste the clippings in an old book and wonder at their exclusion of your name. If your name is never mentioned, never said out loud, erased from the vocabulary, does it change the spelling, the inflection used in speaking the language as a whole?

Everything important happens directly behind you.

I open the scrapbook and page through all my possibilities, while he leans in over my shoulder to share the perception.

"Look here," he tells me, points to a newspaper photograph pasted to a page. "This is when the Seattle high school teachers went on strike. You must have read about that."

"Yes, I lived a couple blocks from a school. Drove by picketers a few times."

"I knew you must have. I told your mother, too. I said Junior must see those striking teachers just about every day."

I flip through the pages until I come to an article about the Miss Native American Contest held in Seattle a couple winters ago.

"I bet you went to see that, didn't you?" he asks me.

"No, no, I didn't."

"But I bet you thought about it, though, enit?"

"Once or twice."

His eyes were closed tight in the reservation October night and the three in the morning fire was the largest in tribal history. He opened

81

his eyes, stared across the flames, into the fire reflecting off the taut skin of the dancers, most naked and those with clothes danced with their eyes. He watched the most beautiful Indian woman in the world swinging her shawl like a shadowy dream, like a fringed promise. He opened his mouth to sing, *to sing for her.*

"Hey, listen up," I ask him. "Is Nadine still around?"

"No, she up and left a while ago. She's out fancydancing on every highway in the country. Should have named her Roadkill."

I put down the scrapbook and look around the room. Everything the same by halves, missing only my definition, my naming. Absence is a powerful name, a powerful magic I feel in all the empty spaces in the house where I have not been in so long. I stand, wanting to touch every wall, to pick up every book, magazine, every piece of furniture and remember it with my hands.

"Did Nadine leave alone?" I ask.

"No, she was shacking up with Frank NoHorses."

"Frank? You mean Fry Bread Frank?"

"Yes, those two together is like a jam sandwich, you know? Just two slices of bread jammed together."

"They'll be back, you think?"

"Sure, all of you come back."

Jesus Christ, Chief Victor yells at the New Year's Eve party, spilling his drink, knocking family photographs off the coffee table. "I was the best goddamned basketball player in Idaho when I was eighteen. It was me and Fast Eddie Garvey and the Cryder brothers, all those white boys at Coeur d'Alene Catholic."

Just after midnight, Jesse WildShoe and Chief Victor get into a fight over who was the better basketball player. Chief picks up a ball and bulls Jesse into the basement door, which breaks, sending them both down the stairs. A crowd of Indians runs to the top of the landing and sees them passed out at the bottom, arms wrapped around each other.

A small Indian boy with half-braids stands in front of the crowd. He is afraid the fall has killed them, broken their necks against the cement of the unfinished basement floor, but they are drunk beyond the body's limitations. It happens that way: a drunk can survive the worst car wreck because his body offers no resistance. Indians are never afraid of a little gravity.

The small Indian boy with half-braids stands at the top of the stairs, listening, waiting for Chief Victor's next, first breath, his eyes blinking involuntarily as Agnes Victor burns flashbulb after flashbulb, *filling a roll of film.*

"Hey," I ask Chief Victor, Senior, remembering those missing photographs. "Where are those pictures of you and Jesse?"

"Burned up in that house fire of '82."

There is so much we can never leave.

"Well," I ask him, "What did you lose in the house fire in '74?"

"I didn't lose anything, but I buried my heart in the ash before it all cooled."

We both smile at the voices we give each other, the way the color of our hair becomes a noun, the dark of our eyes becomes possessive. How does it happen, these same old stories I never heard before but recognize the moment they begin?

I was born in the house fire of '66. Every story I told ashed, collapsed in the house fires of 1967, 1971, 1979. My father disappeared every year, left while the flames stole the very last identification, and every year we found him in a strange kitchen, searching for the proper utensils, the correct ingredients, hoping to cook the last good meal and tell *one more story.*

"Hey," I ask him. "I'm hungry, you got anything to eat around here?"

"Got some fry bread and honey."

"Good enough. Can you heat it up?"

Chief Victor walks into the kitchen, pulls a few pieces of fry bread out of the refrigerator and pops them into the microwave, works the controls without hesitation.

"Nothing ever changes, does it?" I ask him.

"Just a little bit of assimilation, enit?"

I eat the fry bread hot and plain, while my father watches me, his own bread covered in honey and untouched.

"So, what do you want to do tomorrow?" I ask.

"Your mother and sisters won't be back until Monday. Suppose we should chop some firewood."

"What about after that?"

"I don't know."

I finish my fry bread and I look across the table to my father, Chief Victor.

"Listen up," I ask him. "Do you still got that basketball?"

"You mean the only one authorized for reservation play?" he asks me, remembering our old joke.

"Yes, that one."

"Sure," he tells me and finds it in a closet.

We walk outside into the dark, into the back yard where a basket is nailed to a wooden post we both sunk into the ground a thousand stories ago.

"I can't see a damn thing out here," he tells me.

"I can't either."

After a long silence, my father turns to me.

"It's a good thing," he tells me. "It's good to have you home."

He holds the basketball close to his chest, fakes a shot and throws it at me hard. I catch it easily and we both laugh.

"How much you got left?" I ask him, as I take a long jump shot, send the ball arcing noiselessly into the dark.

"Just as much as you," he whispers. "Just as much as you."